REFLECTIONS
OF MY *Life*
GROWING UP
IN *Jamaica*

Reflections of My *Life* Growing UP in *Jamaica*

Sheila Mindola Green

To order additional copies of this book, contact:
Xlibris
1-888-795-4274
www.Xlibris.com
Orders@Xlibris.com
760423

CONTENTS

REFLECTIONS OF MY LIFE GROWING UP IN JAMAICA

Family Makeup

Family Photo of my father, mother seated, sister Dulce standing to the right, Brenda seated on the left and me (age 3) seated to the right.

M y immediate family was comprised of my two parents and their five children. There were Daddy; Mamma; Dulce, the oldest sibling whom I followed; then after me, Brenda; Barbara (Babs); and Don, the only boy among four girls. Although it would appear that I was the second child in this family, I am really the third child, as Mamma had a miscarriage between Dulce and me. I was born in Montego Bay, Jamaica, West Indies, at a private nursing home on Humber Avenue. I imagine the reason for this is that my parents did not want to take any chances after losing baby number 2. Mamma wanted to give me two Christian names and Daddy two different names, so they compromised and gave me all four Christian names: Sheila Mindola Phyllis Delphis. The pastor, Rev. D. A. Morgan, who performed my dedication as a baby, used to joke that he had to memorize those unusual names before the ceremony at Springfield Baptist Church.

Somerton, Saint James

Photo of young Sheila and her mother at age 43

The formative years of my life began in Somerton, where my father was born and where his mother, her sister Adina, and daughter Hattie lived. Because Brenda was born one year and five months after me, I was sent to live with my paternal grandmother, Josephine Ricketts Green, affectionately called Granny Joe. It was felt that this would, as a result, make it easier for Mamma to care for the new baby. Living with my grandmother at that early age, I developed a special bond with her. She was very sweet and tender. She allowed me to hug her and play with the sagging jowls on her neck. She would sing to me about the grandfather clock that went "tick, tock, tick, tock, then stopped, never to go again till the old man died." At Somerton, I was surrounded by loving extended relatives. As the only child in the home, I was at the centre of my grandmother's life until I was returned to my parents in Springfield at around age four.

When I went to Somerton, Aunt Hattie was a young woman still living at home. I bonded with her, and consequently, I am very much like her in terms of housekeeping habits, neatness, and tidiness. Many, many years later in life, when she visited me in New York, I was amazed at how similar we were in those areas. I guess I was her first experience and practice in raising a young child before she left home and went off into the world on her own.

One of my early memories of life in Somerton was being bathed in a wash pan by my grand-aunt, Aunt Adina. She was a very stern lady, and while bathing me, she was not very gentle when scrubbing me. I remember crying for my grandmother to come and bathe me. Granny Joe was on her way somewhere but, upon hearing my cries, returned to bathe me. I do believe the love and attention that I received from my grandmother gave me that sense of confidence and self-assurance that I have always had.

Other memories of Somerton are of playing with my older cousin Dandy and begging her to stay with me when she had to return to her home, leaving me with no other children around. Dandy was the first child and only girl in her family and became one of my favorite cousins. Her mother was Cousin Alice, and she used to ride a mule to Falmouth, where she was a very enterprising businesswoman in the fishing industry.

Aunt Adina was a younger unmarried sister of my grandmother. She was a schoolteacher and had a small basic school where she taught many children at Somerton, including the Honorable P. J. Patterson, the former prime minister of Jamaica. She wore very strong rimless glasses, probably due to poor eyesight. She was a very proper lady, having been raised by the Lowe family—wealthy relatives who lived in Adelphi. The patriarch of the Lowes was the Honorable A. B. Lowe, who was among the first members of the House of Representatives in Jamaica in the 1940s. I attended Aunt Adina's basic school, which was held in a small dirt-floor edifice located up the hill from Granny Joe's at "Top Yard." I used to write on a slate. Education played a very important role in the Ricketts family, and I am told that one of our great-great-grandmothers was a teacher among the slaves and was called govern (probably a shortened form of *governess*).

Photo of my younger paternal aunt (Aunt Hattie) & Photo
of my older paternal aunt- Aunt Carmen (Aunty)

Somerton played an important role in my life and that of my
siblings and cousins. Even after leaving Somerton at the tender
age of four, I would return on a regular basis with my two
paternal aunts, Aunt Carmen (Aunty) and Aunt Hattie, and
Aunt Hattie's children. Both aunts were teachers and would
have long summer holidays off from school. They used this
opportunity to visit their mother. It would be a time for the
cousins, who were more like siblings, to get together. We had
lots of fun. Each day, we had different activities to do. One day,
we might go along with Aunty when she went to pay her respects
to certain members of the community. There were her friends,
Ms. Bella Geohagan; Ms. Winnie, a wealthy housewife; and
Ms. Amy, the Chinese shop owner in the square at Somerton.
Another day, we would visit other relatives, like Aunt Emmy,
my grandmother's sister who was blind and felt us to determine
our growth and development. Aunt Emmy lived in a tiny house
with her daughter, Cousin Edith, and grandchildren, Pearl and
Clinton, who was mentally challenged.

Other days, we would climb from the bottom of the hill (Bottom Yard), where Granny Joe's house was located, to the top of the hill (Top Yard) to visit Aunt May. After climbing up the hill, we would be very thirsty, and we had a ritual of asking Aunt May for water. Although she seemed to be somewhat stern, she would patiently ladle out the water (from a large Spanish jar that kept the water very cold) into a tin mug for each of us. Aunt May was married to Mr. Cunningham, who was a tailor. They had lived in Panama for several years before returning to Jamaica.

She had a trunk full of all kinds of embroidered sheets, pillowcases, and bedspreads that she had acquired in Panama. Aunt May had a twin sister, Aunt Amy, who lived with her husband, Mr. Howard, in Kingston after they returned from Panama. Neither Aunt May nor Aunt Amy had any children.

Aunt Hattie loved to wash clothes, and this seemed to be a daily ritual for her. She would do all the laundry by hand while seated beneath one of the shady trees in the vicinity of Aunt May's house. Aunty would be nearby, while the children ate various fruits and just played around in general. A tap near the entrance to the property from the road made it easy to obtain water for the laundry.

Springfield, Saint James

Springfield was a very special place in the life of my family. Both of my sisters, Brenda and Babs, were born in Springfield. I even remember when Babs was born. She was a seven-month premature baby and was delivered at the teacher's cottage where we lived by the midwife, Nurse Ricketts, who happened to be my father's cousin. I even remember when the doctor arrived in a red car. At that time, I thought that he was the one who had brought the baby. We later discovered that Mamma almost died giving birth to Babs.

Other memories of Springfield at that early age include the funeral of a young boy who had died from eating ackee picked from the tree before it (the ackee) was open and safe to be eaten. I remember watching the procession of the coffin with people walking behind it on the road between the school and church. Until this day, I do not eat ackee, maybe because of this incident and also because Daddy did not allow it to be cooked at home. After Daddy died, Mamma, who liked ackee, started cooking it. I remained loyal to Daddy's wishes.

Another memory of Springfield is that of a storm, seeing the rain pouring outside the window of the teacher's cottage where we lived. I also remember going to a funeral and the burial on a very high hill. I think it was my maternal grandmother Janie's funeral, probably at Saint Alban's Anglican Church— the Solomon family church in the Santa Cruz Mountains in Saint Elizabeth.

My father's close friend in Springfield was the Baptist minister Rev. David A. Morgan, affectionately called DA by his friends. We called him parson. He and my father were avid chess players. Parson, Mrs. Morgan, and their children lived in the manse not too far from the school. Maeve, the only daughter, was one of Dulce's best friends. Her other friends were Grace Ball and Grace Gardener. Nurse Ricketts, the same midwife who delivered Babs, lived in Springfield with her husband,

Papa George. Everybody called him by that name, and I later found out that I was the one who had given it to him. After I got older and my immediate family relocated from Springfield to Kingston, I would continue to visit Nurse and Papa George.

I remember spending the summer holidays with Nurse on one occasion after Papa George's death. I received royal treatment, was given a lot to eat, and had time to read many novels borrowed from the St. Andrew High School library. I would also visit Uncle Easton, my mother's brother; his wife, Aunt Dor; and their children who also lived in Springfield. So I had relatives from both parents living in Springfield. Brenda was born in the house opposite Nurse. Uncle Easton owned a small grocery store located at the square of Springfield. It was located across another store owned by the HoSangs (a Chinese family).

I would often go over to the HoSangs' store to play with Tysin, one of their children in my age group. We would play underneath the counter at the front of the store. After many years, I was able to reconnect with Tysin, now known as Nuke, through the help of her brother Vincent HoSang, a prominent Jamaican millionaire and owner of Royal Caribbean Bakery in New York City.

Kingston

In the midforties, the family moved to Kingston, the capital of Jamaica. It was a big city, and life there was different from the country. I must say that although I lived many years at different times in Kingston while going to elementary school and later to high school, I still think of myself as being from the country. Daddy was the headmaster/principal of Calabar

Elementary School (a large public school in Kingston), and Mamma was a teacher in the infant school. We lived in several different locations in Kingston. The first was at the manse of the East Queen Street Baptist Church, where I remember getting whooping cough and having to drink rat soup. (I am not sure if it was really rat soup.)

Then there was Eleven Victoria Avenue, where we lived in a large house rented from Brenda Smythe, an English woman who operated a music school. Because there were more rooms than we needed, some were rented to Mrs. Doris Hall, her husband, and their two adult nieces. The other rooms were rented to the Tomlinson family. Mrs. Tomlinson worked at Bellevue Psychiatric Hospital, and her children were Monica, Elaine, Barbara, May, and Peter. Mrs. Tomlinson eventually died, and her husband and children relocated to the country.

It was during the time we lived at Victoria Avenue that my only brother, Don, was born on September 24, 1947. I was six years and eight months old, and I vividly remember running home from school at Calabar to Eleven Victoria Avenue to see the new baby. Of course, being the only boy in a family of four girls, he was treated as the little prince of the home.

Daddy started a private school in Kingston named Metropolitan College, but after things did not work out economically, he had to close it. He then returned to the government sector and then went to Linstead, where he became the principal of the elementary (primary) school.

Linstead, Saint Catherine

Mamma did not accompany Daddy to Linstead; instead she found a teaching position at a Catholic school in Kingston and subsequently at another Catholic school in Spanish Town. She even took lessons in Catholicism to better equip herself in their doctrine and philosophy. Brenda, Babs, and I went to Linstead to live with Daddy, while Dulce and Don remained with Mamma in Kingston. I really enjoyed living in Linstead. We lived next to the public hospital and also the Haisley family, which consisted of several boys and only one girl called Glee (although her official name was Lois).

At Linstead, I remember throwing a stray cat into a tank filled with water. I tied the cat with a large stone then threw it into the tank, but because a cat has the reputation of having many lives, it was able to jump out of the water and run away.

Linstead was noted for its sweet oranges, and Daddy would buy them by the hundreds from the farm of a student, Mildred Dixon. Linstead was also noted for malaria caused by the mosquitoes in the region, and we would have to sleep under mosquito nets. There was a saying that just by driving through Linstead, one could get malaria.

Leicesterfield, Clarendon

Our family eventually moved from Linstead to Leicesterfield after about one year, probably because both Daddy and Mamma got teaching jobs there. Leicesterfield is located in the parish of Clarendon and is several thousand feet above sea level. It was very cool, especially at night. We often had to wear sweaters, and Mamma even got a winter coat from one of her brothers in America.

When we moved there, finding suitable housing arrangements created somewhat of a problem. The former headmaster of the school had moved on to become a member of the House of Representatives in the Labour Party. His wife became the acting principal of the school and was resentful of the fact that Daddy was selected as the new principal instead of her. They lived in the house that was the teachers' cottage. However, after much searching for a suitable place, we were able to rent a rather spacious house. It had a drawing room (living room), dining room, four bedrooms, and a bathroom downstairs, but it had no running water and no indoor toilet. Instead, the toilet was an outhouse situated at the back of the house. The kitchen was in another small building to the side of the house. In front of the house, to the left, was a large concrete area called a barbecue, used for drying pimiento. The yard was also spacious, providing lots of room for us children to run around and play, and also for parking Daddy's car—a green four-door Plymouth.

There were two female helpers who did the cooking, washing, and cleaning. Then there was Aston, the yard boy who did gardening, took care of the car, and fetched water from the tank, which was located on a hill in the schoolyard, a short distance from the house. One day, Daddy announced that each one of us had to be assigned a chore (duty). My duty was to do the dusting, and until this day, I enjoy dusting and polishing the furniture.

While we were at Leicesterfield, my cousins—Bev, Madge, and John—came to live with us. They were Uncle Edgar's children, and he felt that they would get a better education with his older brother and family than in Kingston, where they lived.

Because Daddy was the principal of Leicesterfield School and Mamma was one of the assistant teachers, my siblings and I were always expected to behave in an exemplary manner and to be very proper. This was a hard task as we wanted to play and go without shoes like many of the other children. One day, however, when school was usually only kept for a half day on Fridays, Aunty, by then living with us, gave us permission to go to school barefoot. What a pleasure it was to be like the other children! Of course, the stones on the roads were a bit rough on the feet, which were tender and unaccustomed to such abuse.

Another incident that I vividly remember was of me busy chatting away in my class when, all of a sudden, I sensed that someone was looking at me. It was Daddy, who was seated at a desk on a platform located at the centre of the *L*-shaped building—a short distance from my class. I froze and immediately stopped talking, for in those days, only a stern glance from our parents was enough to keep us in line. I remember another occasion when Daddy gave several students intelligence tests to determine our IQ. One of several questions on the tests required that I give as many words as I could in a specific time. I gave so many words that Daddy told me to stop as I had gone way above the limit. I later discovered that I had tested above average.

Each weekend, usually on a Friday, I would drive into Kingston (sixty-four miles from Leicesterfield) with Daddy to take music lessons at Brenda Smythe's music school. My music teacher was Mrs. Adlythe Wilson. She was a tall and slender woman who had two daughters. She was also a smoker, which was quite unusual and somewhat of a rarity among women in those times. I would attend music classes on Saturday for a couple of hours then return to Leicesterfield in the afternoon. Daddy and I would spend Friday night at the home of Mrs. Doris Hall in Kingston. Mrs. Hall worked as a clerk at a clothing store on Luke Lane in downtown Kingston. Her husband was deceased by then, and she lived with her two adult nieces. We met the Halls when they rented a part of our house in Kingston at Eleven Victoria Avenue. The journey into Kingston from Leicesterfield was quite an exciting time for me.

Sometimes Daddy would take some other teachers who wanted to go to Kingston with us. On our return journey to Leicesterfield, we would stop at a roadside seller's place in Clarendon to buy coconut oil and coal made from wood.

Some of the people I remember from Leicesterfield are a couple, Mass Aldin and Miss Lar, his wife. They were small farmers of ginger and coffee. They were kind and welcoming receptive to us and allowed Daddy, Brenda, and Babs to stay with them until the rented house was ready for Mamma, Don, and me to be reunited with the family. There was also Mrs. Murray, one of the teachers who lived near the Baptist church. Then there was Ms. McCalla, another schoolteacher, and her nieces Flora Webley and Monica Thompson.

Bethel Town, Westmoreland

Before Aunty came to live with us at Leicesterfield, she always came to visit us whenever school was closed for holidays. She used to teach at Bethel Town Primary School in Westmoreland, and I once went there to spend some time with her. She lived in a large house situated far back from the road and surrounded by a lot of land. Aunty boarded with the owner of the house, a nice lady everybody called Ms. Liddy. In Bethel Town, there were many ponds with cows grazing in the fields.

Ms. Liddy had a musical powder pot, and I was fascinated with it. One day, she lent it to me, and I walked all around the yard, which was called a common, playing the music from the powder pot over and over. I eventually broke it, and Ms. Liddy was so sweet that she did not make a fuss about it. The strangest thing about Ms. Liddy's yard was that sometimes it would be raining at the gate, but dry and sunny near the house. This meant that the devil and his wife were fighting.

Aunty would always bring gifts for us children when she came to visit. It was rather exciting for us to see what she brought when she opened her suitcase. Most times, there were beautiful dresses made by her dressmaker friend.

Life after the Death of Daddy

After the death of Daddy on the sixth of April 1952, our lives were changed dramatically. I remember when he got sick at Leicesterfield and had to be taken to Kingston by car. Because there was nobody to drive the family car, my uncle Edgar,

Daddy's youngest brother, had to come from Kingston by bus then drive back with both Daddy and Mamma. We later realized that the reason Daddy was unresponsive was that he was in a coma. He was a diabetic and regularly took insulin. He followed a strict diet and would have several small meals daily, including teatime at around 3:00 p.m.

Upon his arrival in Kingston, he was admitted to Kingston Public Hospital but never came out of the coma. Because there were no telephones available to communicate with us at Leicesterfield, a telegram was sent to Aunty stating that she should come to Kingston immediately and bring the children. Of course, she was very apprehensive and deliberately did not pack any clothes for a funeral. By the time we took the bus and arrived in Kingston, we were greeted with the horrible news that Daddy had died.

The funeral was held in Somerton, where Daddy was born and his mother still lived. Many, many people attended the funeral, including a truckload of people from Leicesterfield. Dulce was so brave and even played the organ for the service. Because the rest of us had no white dresses, we wore blue dresses instead. We said our final goodbye to Daddy as he lay in the coffin in a room at Granny Joe's house. We kissed him on his forehead, and I felt his feet, which were very cold. At the graveside, I cried, and my feet buckled under me as the coffin was being lowered into the grave. I was carried away to join Mamma, who was sitting with our cousin, the Honorable A. B. Lowe, in Aunt May's house nearby. Mamma was not allowed to go to the graveside, and she was kept in conversation with Mr. Lowe in order to distract her from the singing taking place at the grave.

When we returned to Leicesterfield, I used to dream that the whole episode was unreal and that Daddy would soon return alive. Mamma had to assume the responsibility of being in charge of herself and her five children. Fortunately, Aunty was living with us and helped a great deal with our care, both physically and financially. Soon we would leave Leicesterfield and move to York Street in Saint Catherine. Brenda and I would go stay with Aunt Hattie in Adelphi while Mamma adjusted to a new life and a new job.

Adelphi, Saint James

Life in Adelphi was great. We lived with Aunt Hattie; her husband, Uncle Wes; and their four children, Dahlia (Dee), Del, Dor, and Brian, whose twin brother Brice died shortly after birth. Brenda and I, having spent summer holidays together with Aunt Hattie and her children at Somerton, found the transition easy. Furthermore, because I had spent my early childhood with Aunt Hattie before she was married, this led to a special bond between us. Although I do not remember, I was told that I was the flower girl at her wedding and had clamored for the cake to be cut before it was ready.

Brenda and I attended Adelphi Primary School, where Uncle Wes was the school principal and Aunt Hattie one of the assistant teachers. As mentioned before, we really come from a family of teachers. Both my parents were teachers as well as two paternal aunts, Aunty and Aunt Hattie. Also, my maternal uncle Easton was married to a teacher, Aunt Dor. (Aunt Dor was the aunt of General Colin Powell, and she always talked about her brother Luther and his family, who lived in America).

Because Aunt Hattie was such a great lover of washing clothes, as soon as we took off our clothes, they were washed and hanging on the line outside to dry. She also believed in feeding us well, and I do think that's where I got my "fat cells." She took great pleasure in combing our hair while we sat on a special bench. Eventually, Mamma decided that it was time for Brenda and me to return to live with her at York Street, a small village in Saint Catherine. The day we left Adelphi, we boarded the Mayflower bus, which went from Montego Bay to Kingston, with everybody outside the school, waving goodbye to us. When we got to the nearest location from the highway to York Street, we were met by some people Mamma had hired to take us on a bicycle. We were home again with Mamma, Babs, and Don. Dulce was away at high school in Kingston.

York Street, Saint Catherine

After the sudden death of Daddy, Mamma moved to York Street, where she became the headmistress of the primary school. The people at York Street were very warm and receptive to us. The day we arrived there, the people came out to greet us and assisted in every possible thing to make us comfortable. Things were hard for Mamma as she was now head of her household and responsible for all the financial needs that Daddy had taken care of over the years. The luxuries that we had taken for granted were no longer the norm. There was only one helper, Brinetta, to do everything for us.

At York Street, we lived in the teachers' cottage and had access to the fruit trees on the premises. There was an otaheite tree that I would climb; I would read books while sitting and eating the fruits from the tree. The pineapples at York Street were plentiful and sweet, so I must have had so many of them that I developed an allergic reaction that flares up whenever I eat too much pineapple. I also suffered from malaria fever while living at York Street. I would be fine during the day, but as night approached, I would shiver and become feverish. I had to take quinine tablets, which were bitter but cured me.

I used to joke about us being on a starvation boat to China. We would devour the supply of groceries bought on the weekends then complain when it was finished by Monday. I even had temper tantrums and rages when I could not get what I wanted. Poor Mamma, she was so overwhelmed with me in my adolescent stage. Anyway, it did not last forever, and I soon became the model daughter in due course. While living at York Street, I developed ringworm behind my left leg and caused the infection to be transferred to my face right between my eyes, probably from scratching it. I was taken to the hospital in Linstead, where they applied an ointment that was so strong it got rid of the infection, but left an ugly dark mark. I was really worried about this situation as I did not want to go to St. Andrew High School with this mark on my face.

After applying various creams, we even resorted to bush medicine from an old lady in the village. Her name was Quattie, and she would come to the house and rub some sort of a poultice made from various leaves. It was very soothing and seemed to help heal it. I believe Quattie acquired this knowledge from her African heritage.

After taking and passing the entrance examination, I was accepted at St. Andrew High School for Girls. This school was one of the most prestigious high schools in Jamaica during that time. The school fees were rather high, but that did not deter Mamma's ambition and desire for all her children to obtain the best possible education. She made the sacrifice to send me to St. Andrew as a paying student. I desperately wanted to be a boarder at St. Andrew, but because of the problem of cash flow, this was not possible. However, she still had to pay boarding expenses for me to stay with relatives or family friends. Thanks to such a mother, I have never felt deprived of emotional or material needs. She is also responsible for the high self-esteem that was given to me and that I have always had.

Kingston, a Second Time

Because Mamma lived in the country, Kingston became home for me a second time as I lived with various families at several locations. First, I lived at the home of the Melbournes. Mrs. Melbourne was a teacher at Calabar Infant School, where Mamma had taught several years before Daddy died. Dulce boarded with the Melbournes while attending St. Andrew High School, so I went to stay there with her before I started school at St. Andrew's in 1953. The Melbourne family consisted of Mr. and Mrs. Melbourne; their two daughters, Carol and Pauline; a son, Paul; and a boarder, Gene Gordon, whose parents resided in America. Both Carol and Pauline attended St. Andrew High School.

Dulce then went to live with the McCartney family on Golding Road in the Cross Roads area of Kingston, and I stayed there too for a short while. The McCartney family consisted of Mr. and Mrs. McCartney; their daughter, Sheila; and two sons, Trevor and Peter. Like Mrs. Milbourne, Mrs. McCartney was a teacher at Calabar Infant School. She was always encouraging me to study and do well in school. I can remember her telling me to remain a child for as long as I could, for once I became an adult, I could never return to childhood except for senility later in life. She would coach me in my studies while she did the laundry in the bathroom.

Before attending school at St. Andrew, I took and passed the first-year pupil-teachers' examination at age eleven. This was quite an accomplishment as this was the route much older students who did not attend high school took as a means of going to teachers' training college.

In 1953, when I started school at St. Andrew's, I first lived with my paternal uncle Edgar; his wife, Aunt Pinky; and their six children, Bev, John, Madge, Dewnette, Carole, and Sharon. They lived in walking distance from the school, so I was able to participate in many after-school activities, such as tennis, netball, hockey, girl guides, Student Christian Movement (SCM), Christian Fellowship (CF), and the drama club. I was an avid reader and would borrow books from the school library and the public library at Half Way Tree. Many of my friends were boarders, and even the teachers thought I was one. I opted to sign up for paid lunch because both the boarders and day girls were fed at the same time after school ended at 1:00 p.m. I even got caught once in the dorm where the boarders lived, but I did not get in trouble as the teacher thought I was there legitimately.

During the six years that I attended St. Andrew's, Brenda and I lived at many places. At one point, we lived with the Taylors at Thirty-Two Truman Avenue, which was also in walking distance from school. Mrs. Taylor had a very structured home, and one of her daughters, June, was in the same form with me at St. Andrew's. Brenda and I had a nice comfortable room with twin beds, and our needs were met in a manner with which we were happy. Lunch would be prepared for us to take to school. Mrs. Taylor was the sister of the wife of our dentist, Dr. Bragg. Dr. Bragg was a family friend and had recommended the Taylors to Mamma. He did not know that Mamma and Mrs. Taylor knew each other from the time when Mrs. Taylor was a teacher at Calabar Infant School. It is interesting to note that the bond formed with three of the teachers (Mrs. McCartney, Mrs. Milbourne, and Mrs. Taylor) at Calabar when Daddy was alive would provide moral support for Mamma when she most needed it.

The years attending St. Andrew's were some of the happiest times of my life. Although no one really taught me how to study, I was able to succeed fairly well academically. I even came first in fourth form (grade) and was promoted from upper 4B to lower 5A. My life at school was one of fun, laughter, and socializing. I was fearless and not afraid to speak up to the teachers, the majority of whom were from England. I made it my business to know girls who were in higher forms and those in lower forms, so I knew many students.

Some of my friends from schooldays are still in my life, and I participate actively in the New York Chapter of the St. Andrew Alumnae Association. Some of the teachers at St. Andrew's who played a great influence in my development were Ms. Pauline Christie, who taught Latin; Ms. Mary Dawson, the headmistress and chemistry teacher; and Mrs. Tess Thomas, who taught English literature, drama, and public speaking. (Later in life, I was able to have Ms. Dawson as a guest in my home in New York and to socialize with Mrs. Thomas when she attended New York University while I was a student there).

In 1956 at age fifteen, I successfully passed in the Second Division, the Overseas School Certificate exam, which was administered by the University of Cambridge. Candidates awarded this certificate had to obtain a grade of credit in at least four of six subjects, including English language. I received credit in seven subjects: English language, English literature, geography, Latin, Spanish (written and oral), mathematics, and biology. In 1957, I took and passed chemistry with a grade of credit. In 1958, I took the Higher School Certificate examination (also from the University of Cambridge) and passed the subjects of English, botany, and zoology. Although I did not pass chemistry at this level and did not obtain the Higher School Certificate, I was able to get credit for those subjects because they were equivalent to the requirements for a bachelor's degree program when I was accepted at New York University.

Sudbury, Saint James

After graduating from St. Andrew's, I returned home to Sudbury in Saint James, where my mother and siblings (except for Dulce) resided. I got a job at Barclays Bank in Montego Bay and worked there for two years before migrating to the United States to study at New York University. Life at the bank was challenging. I would leave Sudbury early in the morning by a van driven by the owner, Mr. Jarrett, taking people to work in Montego Bay. I was always guaranteed a seat in the van no matter how crowded it was. There was a special stool that was saved for me. I remember one morning when Mr. Jarrett came earlier than usual and I was not ready. Despite this, he waited with the passengers sitting in the van until I was ready and then left for Montego Bay. This was the kind of special treatment that I received, and it had contributed to my sense of responsibility to give back to others. To whom much is given, much is expected.

Barclays Bank, Montego Bay

Sheila age 19 with her co-workers from Barclays
Bank, Montego Bay, Jamaica, WI

My job with Barclays Bank was my first full-time job. Prior to this, I had worked during the Christmas holidays at Brown's Drug Store in Montego Bay and part-time at a project with the US government through connections with a teacher at St. Andrew High. At Barclays, we had to wear a uniform consisting of a green skirt and white blouse. Many of the managers were from England, Barbados, and Guyana, and they were mostly white men. I had absolutely no fear of these men.

I remember one day, I was told I had to go to Lucea, which we sometimes had to do. Banking services were provided in Falmouth and Lucea on a once-a-week basis. A group of employees, along with money, would be transported in a chauffeur-driven bank car to provide these services. Most times I did not mind going on these outings as a decent meal would be provided as part of the incentive to go. This time, however, I was not feeling well, so I told the manager that I would be going home instead of going to Lucea. My co-workers were appalled at my audacity to do this. So I went home and told my mother what had taken place. She was worried that I would lose my job. I did not return to work until two days after to make my case more legitimate. I did not get fired.

After working at the bank for two years, I decided to leave Jamaica to attend college in America. I went to the bank manager and told him that I was leaving and asked him to give my job to my sister, Brenda. He agreed.

Church Life

I was raised in the Baptist faith and was dedicated as an infant at the Springfield Baptist Church. After Springfield Baptist, there was East Queen Street Baptist in Kingston. There, I attended Sunday school at an early age and later, as a teenager, was baptized by Rev. Larry Larwood, an Englishman and the pastor of the church. The other Baptist churches that I attended were Leicesterfield Baptist in Clarendon, Jericho Baptist Church in Saint Catherine, and Sudbury Baptist in Saint James. While residing at the home of the McCartneys in Kingston, I went to Saint Luke's Anglican Church with the family, and at the home of my aunt Hattie in Adelphi, Saint James, I attended Marley Anglican Church.

My mother was brought up in the Anglican denomination but joined the Baptist when she married my father. My father was brought up in both the Baptist and Presbyterian church because his mother was Baptist and his father Presbyterian. So although I consider myself Baptist, I am comfortable attending the Anglican and Presbyterian church. My parents were married at the Lockett Avenue Presbyterian Church in Kingston by Rev. Garthshore, the father of Ms. Margaret Garthshore, the early headmistress of St. Andrew High School for Girls.

***

Although I lived for only twenty years in Jamaica before migrating to the United States of America, those early formative years have impacted my personality and character. I still consider Jamaica my home and consider myself a Jamaican even though I have lived many more years away from home.

MEMORIES OF ST. ANDREW HIGH SCHOOL

My connection with St. Andrew High School began a long time before I actually attended school there. It started when my parents were married at the Lockett Avenue Presbyterian Church in Kingston by Reverend Garthshore, the father of the early headmistress of St. Andrew. There was a special bond that existed from the beginning of their marriage, and so even before I was born, there was the plan that their daughters would attend St. Andrew High School someday.

My oldest sister was the first of the four girls to attend St. Andrew, and I can vividly remember the excitement at home when she first won a scholarship to attend St. Hugh's High School and then another to attend St. Andrew's. Naturally, they chose St. Andrew.

I began attending St. Andrew's in January of 1953, the year after my father died. Many friends and relatives of my mother speculated that with only parent and one income to provide for a family of six, I would be unable to attend St. Andrew's. In those days, St. Andrew's was among the most expensive and prestigious schools in Jamaica. Although I did not win a scholarship like my sister, this did not deter my mother's ambition and dream for her children to obtain the best available education no matter what the price or sacrifice. So off I went to St. Andrew's for the next six years from 1953 to 1958 as a paying student.

To compound matters, I had to be boarded with relatives or friends in Kingston because my mother had relocated to the country where she was the headmistress of a primary school. One of my dreams in those days was to be boarded at the school, but when I finally convinced my mother to apply for me to board, it was too late. The school had made a decision to take in younger boarders rather than older students like myself. Because the majority of my friends were boarders, I was always with them whenever possible. I would remain at school for practically the entire day, have lunch at school after classes ended around 1:00 p.m., and then stay on to do my homework and for other after-school activities. I played all three sports offered—tennis, hockey, and netball—and belonged to the drama clubs SCM (Student Christian Movement), CF (Christian Fellowship), and the Girl Guides.

I remember an encounter one day with Ms. Stockhausen, the deputy headmistress, who was so sure that I was a boarder and was only convinced that I wasn't when she checked the typed sheet with the names of the boarders. I even sneaked into the dorms on occasion and got caught one day by Mrs. Hill, the gym teacher. School meant a great deal to me, and I hardly ever missed a day. Whenever there was inclement weather and many students stayed home from school, the boarders would say, "Here comes Sheila Green." They were glad to see me—someone from the outside world.

My memories of my school days are mostly happy ones. I belonged to the Grace Darling House because my sister before me did, and the rule at school was that all sisters belong to the same school house. I imagine this was meant to prevent rivalry and competition within the family. Unfortunately, my attempts at competitive sports, unlike that of my sisters, Dulce and Brenda were not successful I won no prizes was great on enthusiasm and team spirit. So great was my enthusiasm that I fell while jumping hurdles during the heats for sports and broke my right humerus. This caused me to miss about six weeks of school, including the great sports competition day.

During my later school days, there was a pilot project started whereby selected students attended physics classes at Calabar High School. There were four other girls beside myself, and I remember those trips to Calabar well. We had to endure the long walk from the school gate to the classroom while being whistled at by the boys. On the first day of the class, there were rose petals on our chairs. We sat in the front row of the class, hardly ever turning around. We were so self-conscious. Anyway, the course was a success, and we all sat the exam for Senior Cambridge and passed with flying colors.

Many of the friends that I made during my six years at St. Andrew's are still some of the same friends I have today. I clearly remember seeing the "old girls" at their meeting in one of the classrooms at school during the evening and thinking to myself, *When I grow up, I will become an old girl and attend meetings like those.*

Well, I do attend such meetings, but not in Jamaica. Instead we meet in each other's homes on a monthly basis in New York. We are united with a common goal—to assist our alma mater. We not only conduct fundraising events but also attend cultural activities, such as the theatre, dance groups, etc. Coming back to the sixtieth anniversary of the Old Girls Association is indeed a memorable occasion for me. I have often dreamt of being back at school—a place where I spent some of the happiest times of my life. Today, as I visit the school, that dream has become true.

Written by Sheila Green and read at St. Andrew's on July 7, 1991

Sheila (second row seven from right to left) with classmates at St. Andrew High School

Sheila at High School Reunion party in Jamaica, April, 2011

St Andrew Reunion Banquet, Shirley, Sheila and Barbara

The four Green sisters on memory lane visit to Jamaica , April, 2011

FAMILY HISTORY

~~~~~~

Etheline E. Green (Biography)

Mama on her walker in front of steps

Etheline Elethea Solomon (affectionately known as Mamma, Aunt Lyn, Ms. Etheline, Mother Green, and Mamma Green) was born the first of nine children to Charles and Jane Solomon in the village of Good Hope, Saint Elizabeth, Jamaica, West Indies, on May 3, 1909. Both parents placed a strong emphasis on the value and importance of education.

As a young girl growing up, Etheline was a bright and promising student. She was the pride and joy of her parents and, being the first child, was given the best of everything. Upon completing her studies at St. Alban's School, the local elementary school, and successfully passing all three pupil-teacher examinations, she applied for and was accepted at Bethlehem Moravian Teachers Training College in Malvern, Saint Elizabeth.

After graduating in 1931, she started her teaching career. For more than forty years, she taught in the Jamaican public school system, and she served twenty-five years as a principal before her retirement in 1972. She made a profound impact on numerous students who went on to high school and college and made meaningful contributions to society.

On December 23, 1935, Etheline Solomon and Ivor Ethelbert Ricketts Green were united in holy matrimony at Lockett Avenue Presbyterian Church in Kingston, Jamaica, West Indies. The marriage was a happy one and produced five children: four daughters—Dulce, Sheila, Brenda, and Barbara—and a son, Don. Ivor and Etheline operated as a team, devoting themselves to the care and education of their children, with Christ as the head of their home.

On April 6, 1952, Ivor was removed from his earthly life after a brief illness resulting from complications of diabetes. Etheline was left alone with five children ranging in ages from four years to fifteen years. She had to make the transition from being a beloved and pampered wife to one who had to make independent decisions. She courageously tackled the challenge. With God's help and the support of friends and relatives, especially Carmen Green, her sister-in-law, she was able to accomplish a fine job of raising her children. Etheline was an early example of the working mother long before it became fashionable. Not only was she involved with caring for and raising her five children, but along with this, she also administered a school of nine teachers and approximately four hundred pupils. In addition, she was actively involved at the Sudbury Baptist Church as lay preacher, choir director, and organist. She was also president of the local branch of the Jamaican Agricultural Society and represented the community at several national exhibitions and shows at the annual Denbigh Agricultural Show.

In May 1972, after a sudden illness that required further treatment in New York City, Etheline decided that it was time to immigrate to the United States as a permanent resident. At age sixty-three, she still felt energetic and wanted to make a contribution in the area and field that she knew best. So for one year, she taught at a private Lutheran school in Brooklyn, and for the next five years, she worked as a substitute teacher in many day-care centres, also in Brooklyn.

One of the highlights of Etheline's retirement was a three-week trip to Sweden in 1976. She went there to join her daughter Sheila, who, with other graduate students from New York University, was completing an internship program in community health education. Etheline had a wonderful experience in Sweden, often attending some of the lectures with the NYU students.

Upon her return to New York, she had a full program of activities for each day of the week. She attended a weekly seminar on Mondays at the local branch of the New York Public Library and belonged to the neighbourhood senior citizen centre, where she was involved in classes of ceramics, sewing, painting, poetry reading, and cultural field trips. Evidence of her creativity is the handiwork that decorates her daughter's home, which is filled with pottery, macramé hangings, crotchet, and needlework.

Etheline did many other things on her life's journey. She made several visits to Jamaica, often attending Reggae Sunsplash (her son, Don, was one of the founding members of this event attended by music lovers from all over the world). She would visit her daughter Brenda in Canada, staying for several months at a time. Her love of travel stemmed from studying geography—her favorite subject in school. In 1994, she and Sheila, along with friends, visited Israel, where she walked where Jesus walked. In 2000, for her ninetieth birthday present, she went on a Caribbean cruise with Sheila and Barbara. Later that same year, she went with Dulce to Oberammergau, Germany, to attend the renowned Passion play. En route to Germany, she stopped in England to visit her sister Enid in Doncaster, Yorkshire.

Etheline received many awards and recognitions highlighting her various life interests. In June 1996, she was presented with a beautiful plaque from the New York Chapter of Bethlehem Teacher's College Alumni Association for her positive and unselfish contribution to the teaching profession and to the community at large. She was the oldest member of the association and was given a lifetime membership award. In May of 2004, she received a Mother's Day Award from the Friends of Maxfield

Park Children's Home Inc. based on the recommendation of the Hon. Una S. T. Clarke, former New York City council member, with whom she worked at a Brooklyn day-care centre. At Evergreen Baptist Church, she was crowned Mother of the Year and served as president of the Sunshine Group for seniors. She also did volunteer work once a week at Marble Collegiate Church in Manhattan, participating in a group called Cheering where telephone calls were made to lonely homebound people. For more than twenty years, Etheline continued to attend the Glenwood Senior Citizen's Center, which was within walking distance from her home in Brooklyn.

She attended church services at Evergreen until her late nineties but became homebound due to ageing decline, resulting in impaired hearing and vision, several hospitalizations, and medical complications. Despite all these challenges, she still continued to recite passages from the Bible as well as her favourite poem, "The Daffodils" by William Wordsworth, and still had her sound mind.

On Sunday, May 3, 2009, Etheline celebrated her 100th birthday. She always said she wanted to make the century if it was the Lord's will, and she made it. To God be the glory. On December 19, 2009, after a brief illness, Etheline departed from her earthly life and moved on to higher service with her Lord and Saviour Jesus Christ. Mourning her loss were her five children, Dulce, Sheila, Brenda, Barbara, and Don; son-in-law, John McFarlane; daughter-in-law, Velma Green; eight grandchildren; nine great-grandchildren; two brothers, Cecil Solomon and Harry Solomon; sisters-in-law, Julia, Leathea, and Cislyn; two sisters, Enid Harrison (in England) and Pearl

Solomon (in Canada); numerous nieces and nephews; and a host of relatives and friends. We thank God for the gift of her life as we cherish the memories he has bestowed.

Visit to our Mother's Alma Mater in Jamaica

Ivor E. R. Green (Biography)

Daddy Ivor E. R. Green

Ivor Ethelbert Ricketts Green was born on October 4, 1904, in Somerton, Saint James, to Josephine Ricketts-Green and Edward Green. He was the third of six children and the first in his family to attend college. Upon graduating from Somerton Primary School, which included passing the first-, second-, and third-year local examinations, he needed to decide whether he would go on to theological seminary at Calabar or to Mico Teachers' College—both located in Kingston.

The family reports that after much prayer and deliberation, he decided that Mico would be the direction he would take to become a teacher. The oral family history indicates that the teaching profession played an integral part in the Ricketts clan, going back to the days of slavery when a great-grandmother was referred to as governess. This indicates that education was a very important value in this family.

Ivor was a studious child, and when his siblings would be involved in doing chores in the home, he would be seen reading his books. His mother had to continue caring for her six children as a single parent upon the death of her husband. She was a major force in encouraging young Ivor in his studies. He graduated from Mico College with first-class honours and was an avid player of cricket and soccer.

On the twenty-third of December 1935, Ivor married Etheline Solomon at the Lockett Avenue Presbyterian Church in Kingston. He met Etheline at a church function in his hometown of Somerton, where she was teaching. She had a beautiful singing voice, and the family story states that it was love at first sight.

Etheline was also a close friend of Ivor's sister Carmen, who lived in Somerton at the time. The courtship lasted for some time as Etheline was not interested in marriage, but eventually she relented.

The first school job assignment for both Ivor and Etheline was at Pike Elementary School in Manchester. Their first child, Dulce, was born a year later, but they left soon after because the baby's health suffered in the cool climate of the Manchester hills. They then went to Springfield School in the Parish of Saint James, where Ivor was principal of the boys' school and Etheline the principal of the girls' school. While they were at Springfield, they had three more children—Sheila, Brenda, and Barbara.

Mamma with three of her daughters, Dulce, Sheila and Barbara

Ivor was not only a highly respected and well-loved teacher but also an active member of the affiliated Baptist church where he was a lay preacher and choirmaster who staged ambitious cantatas and concerts, attracting enthusiastic audiences to this country church. He had a close relationship with Rev. David Morgan, the pastor of the church, and as avid chess players, they shared and emanated contagious joy. After several glorious years in Springfield, Ivor and Etheline relocated to Kingston. Soon they were delighted to have their only son, Don, delivered at Jubilee Hospital located in Kingston.

Ivor became the principal of Calabar Elementary School, one of the largest elementary schools in Kingston. The school was affiliated with East Queen Street Baptist Church, where the family worshipped. Ivor's next venture was to open a private school, Metropolitan College, but due to financial challenges resulting from students' inability to pay for tuition, he decided to return to public school education.

He taught for one year at Linstead Primary School then moved on to Leicesterfield School in Clarendon.

Photo of Mamma and Sheila after church

On April 6, 1952, Ivor died in Kingston after a sudden and brief illness resulting from type 2 diabetes.

Ivor made exceptional impact on the vast number of students he taught and indeed on the wealth of people he met during his short life of forty-six years. As a self-starter, he used his college foundation to propel him to teach himself Spanish, and even Greek, and continuously emanated his passion for learning. Besides teaching woodwork and agriculture, included in the school curriculum, he taught piano and gave private lessons, which resulted in success for students who otherwise would not have afforded the national examinations. Ivor accomplished much and will always be remembered for his enthusiastic generosity, his winning smile, his brilliance, his charming personality, and the love he showed to his fellow man.

Don and his grandson Andrew

Sheila Green

Mamma and Don at Babs' apartment in Brooklyn

Mamma and Miss Dawson, St. Andrew head
mistress at 5515 Avenue H, Brooklyn, NY

Mamma on vacation in Israel

Mamma with Babs and Sheila on Mother's Day 2001

Green Family Reunion in Canada, 2001

Sheila and Mamma pose in front of 5515 Avenue H, Brooklyn, NY

MY TRIP TO THE SOVIET UNION

"Why did you choose Russia of all places to visit?" everyone asks. It all began with a telephone call in the middle of the night. It was my girlfriend Vena calling from England, and though it was six o'clock in the morning there, it was only 1:00 a.m. for me in New York. "Sheila," she said, "would you like to go with me to Russia? My job has a travel club, and we plan to go there for a reasonable fare." My first reaction was "Of course, I'll go!" Caution, however, prevailed, and instead I suggested that she send me the relevant information, such as price, itinerary, dates, etc.

The expected letter arrived in the mail shortly after, and I reluctantly decided that I could not go due to other factors in my personal life. Some months later, when I realized that the expected events had not materialized, I took the plunge, called Vena, and told her to count me in. From there on, I took positive steps towards making the trip a reality. The total cost for the trip included round-trip airfare between England and Russia, land transportation in Russia, three meals per day, and two city tours.

The rest was very easy. A cheap round-trip fare on the airline (People's Express) to London made the overall cost of the trip too good to miss.

For months before the planned event, I corresponded with Susan Williams, the travel club organizer in England. She was extremely helpful, and I was thoroughly impressed with her efficiency and competency in handling the pretrip arrangements. She suggested that I obtain my visa for Russia in the United States rather than with the group in England. This involved phone calls and correspondence with the Soviet Consulate in Washington, DC, and the Intourist office in New York. Finally, my visa arrived late and very near the departure date from New York, causing me some anxiety. The instructions that came with the visa indicated that I should make sure all the information required was correct, as there could be serious problems when I arrived in the USSR. Needless to say, all the information on the visa was written in Russian, and I had no opportunity to find out whether it was correct. All I could recognize was my birthdate and the dates of arrival and departure there, as even my name was in Russian.

The day of departure to the Soviet Union finally dawned on a Saturday in England, when Vena and I boarded Britannia Airlines, flight BY058A at Gatwick Airport, bound for Moscow. The flight departed on time at exactly 10:05 a.m. It was a comfortable flight, which took just a little over three hours, and then we landed at Sheremetyevo Airport at 4:15 p.m. (Moscow time). As we approached for landing, there was a feeling of excitement and tension in the air. Through the windows, I could see the Moscow skyline with modern-looking skyscrapers in the distance. Below was a vast expanse of land with wooded forests of birch trees and frozen lakes. I put on my coat and hat, getting ready for what I felt would be freezing cold weather, only to be pleasantly surprised otherwise.

All around the airport was the presence of the military; soldiers in attractive uniforms seemed to be everywhere. I was intrigued by their faces, which seemed to be a mixture of Caucasian and Oriental features. All throughout my visit, I was fascinated with the evidence of the various ethnic groups of people. While they were busy looking at Vena and me (there were very few black people there), I was also watching and observing them.

The airport appeared quite large and modern although it seemed poorly lit, as if they were conserving electricity. We all waited in queues as we prepared to face the ordeal of immigration and customs. The information manual that Susan had given us forewarned us to be patient (*nicheve*) and to expect long, tedious delays everywhere. After what seemed like ages, I came face-to-face with an immigration officer looking at me from behind a glass cubicle. This was a nerve-racking experience for me, caused for the most part by fear of the unknown. The young officer looked at my passport and visa, looked at me, then again at the documents, saying nothing the entire time. I didn't know what to think or expect. All sorts of thoughts were running through my mind, especially the warning about everything being correct on the visa. In addition, the pictures for my passport and visa might have seemed different because I was fifteen pounds lighter when I took the more recent visa picture.

"Sheila," he said haltingly. "Are you Sheila?"

"Yes," I said nervously and proceeded to rattle on about how I had been on a diet, therefore that was the explanation for the difference in my appearance in the pictures. There was no indication whether or not he understood what I was saying. I got the feeling that this was all part of the intimidation process practiced on all incoming foreigners. Furthermore, here I was, a black woman with a US passport, born in the Caribbean and traveling with a British group! I wonder what he was thinking. I later discovered that a young Brazilian man on the same flight was put through some grueling interrogation upon entry because of some discrepancies in the currency he declared versus what he had on him. It was a simple oversight on his part but enough to create suspicion.

After immigration came customs. We had been advised through Susan's manual and again by an announcement on the plane to leave behind any Western literature, newspapers, magazines, etc., on the aircraft before disembarking. They would only be confiscated by the Soviet authorities. Somehow the officers in the customs area did not seem as intimidating as those in immigration. Our luggage passed through what seemed to be an x-ray machine and was viewed on a monitor. We were required to declare all currency, jewelry, and Bibles being carried into the country so that upon departure, all purchases with their receipts could be compared with an entry declaration form. My general feeling was that all would be well as long as we followed instructions and obeyed their laws.

I was amazed that not everybody acted accordingly. On several occasions during the trip, we were asked not to take any photographs using a flashbulb. This was usually inside museums, palaces, trains, etc. Would you believe there was always someone who invariably proceeded to break the rule? I guess we capitalists are not about to conform. Speaking of capitalists, one day, after the Intourist guide had made some reference to the group as capitalists, someone asked her a question about the buildings in Moscow painted in drab colours. He felt that brighter colours would be more pleasant and tended to last longer. At that point, the guide asked him if he was American. When he said that he was not but persisted as to her reason for asking, she said somewhat sarcastically, "Oh, the Americans are always so logical." Many times, I would hear other references about capitalists voiced in negative overtones; then I stopped and thought, *Don't we do the same about communists?* It was really a learning experience to face the obvious fact that the Russians are people just like us in the West, with similar prejudices and hopes for peace and a better world. Furthermore, it was interesting to learn that only a small percentage of the Soviet people actually belong to the communist party. The majority are occupied with the daily task of survival and living.

After the airport encounter, we left by bus for our hotel room at the Intourist Hotel, which is within walking distance of Red Square. We had a meal in a restaurant located in the hotel and then decided to get a head start on our guided tour of Moscow scheduled for the following morning. We wanted to venture out and see Red Square at night; however, just before leaving the hotel, I had an annoying experience. The shops in the hotel lobby were closed for business, but we were able to look at the various items displayed through the glass enclosures. Suddenly I felt someone touch me from behind. I quickly spun around to see a middle-aged man who seemed to have had too much to drink and was obviously making a pass at me. I yelled at him to get away. It had happened so fast that Vena only realized what had happened when I told her. I felt that here we were, two independent black women, being accosted merely because we were without male escorts. I was outraged, so much so that we returned to the hotel room for our umbrellas, armed and ready for any further attacks as we set off for Red Square.

In order to reach Red Square, we had to use an underground passageway as the streets were so wide it was impossible for pedestrians to cross safely. My first impression of the city was its hugeness. The buildings seemed large and imposing. Even the people looked large as well. It soon became clear to me that our general use of the word *Russians* is not an accurate one because the Russians are only one of the many ethnic groups of people in the Soviet Union. This vast country, which has eleven different time zones, consists of fifteen provinces and several different ethnic groups with a little over 50 percent of the total population; and there are other groups, such as the Ukrainians, Georgians, Moldavians, Armenians, etc.

In Red Square, it was an awesome experience to stand in the place that we often saw on television and where the might of the USSR is displayed on May Day. At the entrance to the mausoleum with Lenin's tomb were three guards who change shifts every hour, on the hour, twenty-four hours per day. The soldiers march with goose-step precision, with rifles slung over their shoulders, and as the hour strikes from Spasskaya Tower, the new guards take over the watch for the next hour. On either side of the entrance to the mausoleum, there were several floral bouquets, which bridal parties bring and leave as part of their wedding ritual. Elevated marble stands on either side of the entrance are the viewing stands where the Soviet leaders watch the May Day parade and other important events. The famous Saint Basil's Cathedral, with its unique architecture, was a beautiful sight to see. Even at 10:00 p.m. that night, there were many, many people walking around Red Square, and we were told later that it was safe to be there without fear of being mugged (I don't know about now).

On the next day, which was a Sunday, I woke up at 6:00 a.m., my sleep pattern somewhat affected because of the various time changes. First, I had lost six hours in the New York / England daylight savings time difference then three more hours between England and Moscow. The jet lag was to affect me throughout the trip, so whenever I sat down for too long, I tended to doze off.

As I mentioned before, the tour provided us with three meals per day, and we had them in the restaurant located at the Intourist Hotel. I found the food to be wholesome though not necessarily of gourmet quality. There was a lot of bread—black bread and white bread, cold cuts of every kind, eggs, meat, fish, pastry, and ice cream, reputed to be very good. We were told to avoid the water, but they had some delicious pear and peach drinks, as well as lemonade and beer. Naturally, I had to have black and red caviar with dinner on several occasions. Some of the other highlights of the Moscow visit were the sightseeing trip to the Kremlin; the Pushkin Museum; the Metro (subway); the Halls of Economic Achievement, where we saw models of their space achievements; a Russian folklore performance; to a Beriozka shop; and the famous Moscow Circus.

The Kremlin visit involved a walking tour. The Kremlin is really a city within a city, and it is surrounded by sturdy walls with several watchtowers. Inside are several cathedrals that have been converted into museums. We went into the Cathedral of the Assumption, the main church of the Kremlin that was built in the fifteenth century. The walls inside the church are covered with magnificent paintings and icons, examples of the finest of Russian church architecture. The throne of Ivan the Terrible remains within. The centre of the Kremlin is called Cathedral Square and is the oldest square in Moscow. The Tsar Bell, said to be the largest bell in the world, weighs two hundred tons, and the Tsar Cannon, also the largest in the world but never fired, was pointed out to us by the Intourist guide. We were told constantly that things in the Soviet Union were the largest and best in the world.

The Palace of Congresses, a modern building made from marble, glass, and aluminum, reminded me of the United Nations building in New York. We did not go inside but were told it had eight hundred rooms and halls, five storeys connected by staircases and fourteen escalators, and an auditorium with a capacity of six thousand. An unusual feature is that the building is sunk fifteen meters into the ground.

The tour of the Metro was simply unbelievable. The high-speed escalators descending to the underground are extremely steep and exceptionally deep. People suffering from hypertension were advised not to go. The fare was a mere five kopeck, regardless of the distance traveled. It was a spectacular sight to see the displays of the finest Soviet architects, sculptors, and artists. The chandeliers and sheer opulence were mind-boggling. This was certainly the reverse of capitalism in that the best was provided for the workers.

Only a few of us elected to go to the Pushkin Museum. The majority opted to go to Lenin's Museum. I had had enough of Lenin by then. His statue and presence dominates all of Moscow. Furthermore, we arrived in Moscow near the end of April and close enough to the upcoming May Day parade. In addition, there would soon be celebrations for the fortieth anniversary of the end of World War II. The streets were decorated with red flags at every street corner and light post, and there were more posters of Lenin, Marx, and Engels. It seemed evident to me that red is the favourite colour of the Soviets.

Getting back to the Pushkin Museum, which I enjoyed thoroughly, I must mention that in every building we entered, we had to check our coats at no charge. It is considered to be poor taste to walk around with your coats while indoors, especially because the interior of the buildings are kept warm and comfortable. At the Pushkin, I saw some of the great masterpieces by Botticelli, El Greco, Rembrandt, Cezanne, Gauguin, Manet, Monet, Van Gogh, and many others. The tour guide was extremely knowledgeable and articulate in English. Furthermore, she was able to guide us much better than had we been on our own.

The USSR Exhibition of Economic Achievement consisted of several exhibits spread out in buildings on about 550 acres of land. Among the pavilions was one with the achievements of space and technology in the USSR. Another housed the achievements of arts and crafts done by children in vocational schools from several provinces. Unfortunately, the arts and crafts were on display only and not for sale. The Moscow Circus and Russian folklore performance were both magnificent, and I was especially thrilled by the singing and dancing of the folklore troupe. The female singing voices had a high, reedy sound usually associated with the Orient. Their costumes were very beautiful and depicted several ethnic groups of the USSR.

"What are Beriozka shops?" you might ask. These are stores where you can use only foreign (hard) currency, and for the most part, they are located in hotels. It seemed rather unfair that these stores provide luxury shopping denied to the ordinary Soviet citizen. I was able to purchase several items, such as interesting ethnic souvenirs as well as amber jewelry and woolen scarves, for rather reasonable prices. There was no need to haggle over prices, which are the same throughout the USSR. Because the tour was geared more towards the cultural sights, there never seemed to be enough time for shopping for either Vena or myself. We managed, however, to do pretty well despite this drawback.

A visit to their largest department store (GUM), where only Russian currency may be used, opened up another side of Soviet Russia for us. Here we mingled with the ordinary Soviet citizen away from the segregated and orchestrated tour setting. The system used for paying for merchandise seemed geared towards long lines and waiting periods. You must first select what you want to purchase, wait in line to pay for it, and then wait in line again to pick up your merchandise. This system obviously causes people to spend an inordinate amount of time waiting in lines. They seemingly accept it as a way of life, and everywhere we drove, we would see long lines of people waiting outside stores, shops, and buildings.

Although there were cars, buses, and tram cars with overhead electrical connections, I noticed that in Moscow, there seemed to be an absence of the kind of traffic jams that you associated with a large metropolis. From what I gathered, cars are not easily available to the ordinary citizen, and there are long waiting lists for people to buy one. Consequently, the kind of air pollution associated with the presence of exhaust fumes from cars, trucks, buses, etc., is missing. The subway system is cheap and extensive so that public transportation makes up for the lack of private transportation.

The Hotel Intourist, where we stayed in Moscow, is a large modern hotel with somewhat of an impersonal air. Each floor has a floor lady (*deshurnaya*) who guards the comings and goings on the floor. Unlike my expectations, they were not all old ladies, and most of them were young and pleasant. Despite the language barrier, I was able to arrange for them to iron my clothes through the use of sign language.

Because of my lack of knowledge of the Russian language, I was not willing to venture off on my own, and so I mostly stayed with the group on the guided tours. The prices of jewelry and souvenirs were very reasonable, and I took advantage of them all. It was a rather strange experience, however, not to be able to read the street signs, or anything else for that matter. Even in the subway, we had to count the number of stops rather than try to decipher the Cyrillic alphabet of the Russian language. I must say that there was indeed a certain sense of adventure to be there.

I felt that in Moscow, I was definitely in a Soviet city, as opposed to Leningrad (Saint Petersburg), which has more of a European flavour. Moscow was like no other place that I had ever visited. The three days there felt like three weeks; we had covered so much ground. Maybe in another couple of days, I would have been willing to travel alone on the subway and explore elsewhere. The Intourist guide assured us that if ever we got lost, there would always be someone willing to help.

After a while, certain landmarks did become familiar, and with this came a lessening of the strangeness and tension. There seemed to be nobody following us around, and maybe our room was not bugged after all. I did not forget, however, that no matter how nice and friendly the Intourist guides were, they were probably KGB informers. We secretly dubbed the Intourist guide in Moscow "Moscow Annie." She wore rimless glasses and looked like the classical daughter of the Soviet revolution. She was very knowledgeable and informative but maintained a certain severity and distance from us all. She did not laugh or smile with the spontaneity of some of the other guides. She even quizzed us on some of the information she had given us, to check whether we had been paying attention.

The next stop on this exciting visit to Russia was the visit to Leningrad. We left Moscow at about 1:30 p.m. by train and arrived in Leningrad some twelve hours later, near midnight. We had prepared for a long train ride, but the journey was even longer than the estimated travel time. The ride was fairly comfortable, and the time went by quicker than I would have expected. All the members of the group were assigned to one car, so again we were isolated from the Soviet people. We saw very little of them except for those occasions when they passed through our car on their way to the dining car or elsewhere. We spent the travel time eating from our boxed lunches prepared by the hotel in Moscow, playing card games and scrabble, reading, and looking at the landscape through the windows.

Vena and I ventured to the dining car where we communicated with the waitress in sign language. (I was getting good at this.) Because we were unable to read the menu, we remembered that beef stroganoff was a Russian dish and so ordered it. The price of the meal was phenomenally small, and it was quite enjoyable.

At several stations, the train would stop long enough for passengers to walk about outside and buy from the vendors congregated nearby. It reminded me of the train rides of my childhood in Jamaica, when local vendors would do similar selling to passengers at each train station on the journey between Montego Bay and Kingston. Vena and I did not get off the train as we were content to people-watch through the windows. The landscape on the whole was rather bleak as winter had not completely gone. The dachas (summer cottages) seemed to be deserted; however, you could see the buds on the trees signaling the arrival of spring.

Despite the late arrival in Leningrad, most of the group opted to have the sumptuous meal prepared and awaiting us at the hotel. This hotel was rather grand and modern-looking, Finnish architecture and design. The service was excellent and better than in Moscow. The city of Leningrad, with its close proximity to the Scandinavian countries, seemed rather charming and beautiful. It is connected by several bridges over many rivers, the largest being the Neva River, which flows into the Gulf of Finland. This city is the second largest in the USSR and was very impressive, with its beautiful churches and the Hermitage Museum, one of the most beautiful and famous museums in the world.

The first day in Leningrad was rainy and overcast and seemed cooler than Moscow. Because we had all gone to bed very late after the long trip from Moscow, everybody on the sightseeing tour that morning was tired and sleepy. The Intourist guide could not understand our seeming lack of interest and our apathy. Someone began to snore audibly, adding insult to injury. It was then that we told her the reason for the malaise and apparent indifference. After a good laugh, some of us were able to wake up sufficiently to take in and enjoy the sights of the city.

Our tour guide was Irina, and she was young and attractive-looking. One of the group members complimented her on her smart appearance, but instead of accepting the compliment graciously, she asked somewhat defensively if we thought Russians were incapable of being attractively dressed. Contrary to the stereotype of the dowdy Russian female, I saw several attractive and elegant women in the subway, on the streets, and at the theatre. Of course, there were the dowdy ones as well, with their scarves tied over their heads in peasant style.

The presence of women as labourers was very evident. We saw them working in construction, sweeping the streets, painting buildings from scaffolds, and old ones in museums watching and keeping guard over their art treasures. We got the sense that people watched out for the care and protection of Soviet property, which they were proud of and protective of as well. The subways were spotlessly clean, and nowhere did we see anyone smoking in them. There was no evidence of graffiti anywhere. It was nice to see older people being productive in even the smallest way and not discarded as in some other urban societies. They really seem to see themselves as the guardians of the state property and appear to occupy positions of respect from their fellow comrades.

At the hotel in Leningrad, I went to the beauty salon for a manicure. I observed that the women there were somewhat subdued; there was no happy, spontaneous laughter that I associate with a beauty salon. Of course, this could simply be a cultural factor; besides, my presence could have caused it. The salespeople in the Beriozka shops were all women, and they were generally not friendly and lacked the sensitivity for tourist relations. We felt that we were imposing when we inquired about prices of merchandise we were interested in buying. Tourism, in my opinion, is not developed in the Soviet Union. They have a long way to go.

Before leaving Moscow, the group was told that we had the option to visit the town of Novgorod as a side trip from Leningrad. This was the first time in a long time that this town was opened up to tourists, so we grabbed the opportunity with great enthusiasm. We had to submit our passports as a special visa was needed to go there. Novgorod is an old Russian town that is very authentic in that much of the culture was preserved from the usual invasions by foreigners in the past.

At the museum there, we saw lovely icons and paintings reflecting the works of original Russia. An old monastery was being restored and was to be converted into a museum. There was a war monument with an eternal flame, and high school students stood watch, changing guard every fifteen minutes. They marched with similar goose-step precision as the guards before Lenin's tomb in Moscow. We were told that the rifles that the children carried were not loaded. Bridal parties also brought floral bouquets to leave by the monument and eternal flame. On the way to Novgorod, we drove by several communities with dachas reflecting uniquely different styles and colours. It gave the countryside a picturesque and pleasing atmosphere. An outdoor museum had several wooden houses, depicting the styles of pre-revolutionary Russia.

The day in Novgorod showed us another side of Russia—that of a more rural setting, as opposed to the big cities of Moscow or Leningrad. There never seemed to be a crowd of people anywhere. Maybe they were indoors at work because this was during the daytime on a weekday. Lunch was provided for us at the local Intourist hotel, and the food was plentiful and attractively prepared. The weather was pleasant, bright, sunny, and comfortably spring-like. It was rather a surprise to discover when we returned to Leningrad that evening that it had snowed there. This could perhaps explain why several people were still wearing their boots as well as fur coats and hats. I would have looked to explore the possibility of buying a fur coat, but this would have meant breaking away from the tour group to venture off on my own. Other members of the group who had been to Russia before did so and had interesting experiences of interacting with Soviet people.

Other sightseeing activities in Leningrad consisted of a tour of Saint Isaac's Cathedral, the palace of Catherine the Great, a Russian Museum, a Metro trip, the ballet, and the Piskaryovskoye Memorial Cemetery. The latter is the site of the unmarked graves of the many thousands of Russians who died in the historical nine-hundred-day siege of Leningrad. Saint Isaac's Cathedral was converted into a museum in 1931, and the architecture and style are believed to be inspired by Saint Peter's Basilica in Rome. It is also one of the world's largest churches. The walls and ceilings are covered with religious paintings that depict stories from the Bible. I was deeply saddened to see such a beautiful church no longer a hallowed place of worship. There were tourists from the USSR, from other communist countries, and from the West. I felt that surely something spiritual must have been transmitted to all those who visited.

Catherine's Palace gave credence to the Russian love of fine Italian workmanship and artistry. It is another of the Italian Rastrelli's masterpieces, with its ornate furnishings restored to show the elegance and wealth with which the Russian aristocracy lived while the masses starved and died.

On the last day of our visit, it snowed again in Leningrad, but not for long; and it did not stick to the ground. The last sightseeing event was the visit to the Russian Museum in the morning. This was very interesting and delightful, and after the other museums with the works of European artists, we now saw only those of Russian artists. The paintings were by artists from the twelfth century up to the nineteenth century. It was also interesting to watch the huge crowd of visitors, including Soviet families with their children, as well as Young Pioneer groups. Every moment of this trip had been spent in a worthwhile manner.

Our flight to London was scheduled for the afternoon, and as we left the hotel, I felt that it was too soon. There were still other things that I wanted to see and do. The officials at the airport in Leningrad did not seem as intimidating as those in Moscow. Maybe it seemed that way because we were leaving. However, I was the only member of the group asked to open my suitcase for inspection. It seemed that some souvenirs I had wrapped in tissue paper must have shown up on the x-ray monitor and created some suspicion. They seemed to know exactly what they were looking for and went immediately to that area of the suitcase. As I knew that I had nothing to hide or to be guilty of, I was not afraid, although I was glad when it was over, and they closed up the suitcase.

After the luggage was checked in, we still had time for some last-minute shopping in the airport shops. Then the flight was announced for departure, and we headed for buses to take us to the plane parked some distance away from the main building. In true Soviet style, there were armed soldiers stationed by the plane to watch us as we embarked. It was a strong reminder that the freedom to leave the Soviet Union does not exist for all. I breathed a sigh of relief as the plane took off, and shortly after, the pilot announced that we had left Soviet airspace and were flying over Finland.

When I arrived at Gatwick Airport in England and the immigration officer stamped my passport, I realized that there was no evidence in it that I had been to the Soviet Union. The

Russians do not stamp your passport as most countries do; instead they issue a visa, part of which they take when you enter the country and the other part they retrieve when you leave. Except for the souvenirs, pictures, and memories, it seemed as if the entire visit to Russia had never happened, and I had awakened from a dream.

(Note: Leningrad has reverted to the name Saint Petersburg.)

NYU INTERNSHIP REPORT ON HEALTHCARE IN SCOTLAND

The four weeks spent as part of the group of New York University students in Scotland have been an invaluable learning experience for me. It has vividly brought to light how much more I need to know about the healthcare system in the United States. During this visit, my goal was to take a closer look at the health system in Scotland and learn from this experience.

Whenever one observes another system, it is only natural to make references to and comparisons with the system with which one is more familiar. So although comparisons were inevitably made with the United Sates, the aim was not to find out which was better or worse but simply to gain knowledge and a better understanding of the systems.

Scotland is a country of five million people and is part of the United Kingdom of Great Britain. Two-thirds of the people live in one-third of the land in the region between the largest cities of Glasgow and Edinburgh. There are also two contrasting types of lives in the same country. One is the Highlands to the North, which is thinly populated, and the other in the Lowlands, which is rural and more thickly populated. The city of Glasgow alone has one million inhabitants. Scotland has been a country from which many of its people have immigrated to other countries, and Scots are to be found all over the world. Glasgow is eight hundred years old and was once a great ship-building city, among other industries. There has, however, been great decline in the industries, and the city has been faced with the dilemma of some of the worst slums in Western Europe. The city of Edinburgh was the centre of academic learning, banking, insurance, and religion. It is still a great architectural city and is one of the most beautiful in all Europe.

When one thinks of a health system and Scotland, the first thought that comes to mind is that of socialized medicine and the National Health Service. The National Health Service was established in 1948 in order to create a comprehensive system of healthcare after growing social pressure and concern in Britain. After some twenty-five years, the organization has been reorganized, and on April 1, 1974, a new structure was introduced in Scotland. Fifteen health board areas have a total of forty-eight local health councils, which represent consumer interests.

In my opinion, this is an excellent means of maintaining the interest of the community as a whole rather than a particular view of the group or organization from which they are appointed or nominated. On the other hand, there is a lack of quality control for healthcare and medical personnel that are prevalent in the United States.

Within the National Health Service are hospital doctors or specialists, family doctors or general practitioners, dentists, ophthalmic medical practitioners, opticians, dispensing opticians, retail pharmacies, and nursing staff. Medical services are free for all, and dental services have a small fee attached.

I found the system of the general practitioner working, along with the health visitor, the district nurse, and the social worker, to be an excellent one. Patients may remain with the same general practitioner even if they relocate to another part of the city or town. As a result, the GP has an intimate knowledge of the patients. The role of the health visitor is an important one where health education is concerned. She is a nurse who makes domiciliary visits and is a link between the GP and the patient at home.

Despite the existence of the National Health Service, the life expectancy of Scotland has not been raised that much. Nor do the poor utilize the NHS as well as the middle class. This may be due to many factors among them, such as the presence of the rigid class structure, which has an undermining effect on the delivery of healthcare. The classes IV and V people do not obtain the maximum benefits as reported and obviously have a poor educational background. The health services agencies are therefore challenged with the problem of changing these situations.

The visit to the Woodside Health Centre in Glasgow gave a clear picture of the group practice of general practitioners and the availability of comprehensive health services in one location. It was very pleasing to learn that there were no waiting lists for a patient to see a doctor. Usually, an appointment could be made early in the morning to see the doctor that same day.

My Travel Experiences
in Sweden

~~~~~~

O ne of the most interesting and richly rewarding experiences that I have had was my travel experience in Sweden. The opportunity arose for me to visit Sweden as part of the internship program towards obtaining a master's degree in community health education from New York University. The internship consisted of spending four weeks in Scotland and four weeks in Sweden observing and working in a healthcare facility, and for this experience, I gained twelve credits towards completing the degree. This article will describe and share with you some of the highlights of my stay in Sweden.

My home away from home for the four weeks in Sweden was a two-storey house called the Villa. It was located on the hospital premises in Tierp—a small town located about 120 miles to the north of Stockholm. The Villa, which was normally occupied by nursing students and others connected with the hospital, was unoccupied during my stay, as they were on vacation. I would like to mention that my sixty-seven-year-old mother joined me in Sweden for three out of my four weeks in Tierp. It was a real treat for her, and she shared some of my experiences there as well as some of her own. There was another NYU student doing her internship along with me, so there were three "Engleskas" at Tierps Sukhus och Halsocentral (Tierp Hospital and Health Center).

One of my first experiences there was to wake up at 2:00 a.m. to see daylight streaming through the windows. This was a strange and awesome experience, but luckily for me, this did not interfere with my ability to return to sleep. Along with the working and learning experience was the opportunity to meet with the Swedes in an informal setting, both at work and in their homes. Although many people spoke English, it was a strange feeling to be completely surrounded by people speaking a language that sounded like nothing I knew. They often commented on the fact that I seemed to be concentrating and listening intently to their speech on those occasions that they lapsed into Swedish in my presence. Believe it or not, I very quickly began to understand what they were saying, maybe from their rhythmic intonations, gestures, or body language.

My first assignment at the hospital was with the district nurse, Margaretha, who took both the other NYU student and me on her visit to her homebound patients who were unable to come into the hospital clinic. In this way, we got another glimpse at the lives of persons from varying social and economic backgrounds. We visited a so-called poor family whose home was spotlessly clean and comfortably furnished. It was owned by an old couple who lived in the countryside near Tierp. The husband was bedridden, blind, and suffering from diabetes. They were delighted to have foreign visitors in their home. Margaretha wanted to show us some more of the Swedish countryside, so she took us along an unpaved back road where we stopped and picked wild strawberries and blueberries. What a delight! It was so calm and peaceful there, with not a trace of pollution in the air. Margaretha then took us to her home for lunch and introduced us to her fourteen-year-old son, who was home from school on summer vacation. When we were ready to leave, she presented us each with a painted wooden hen that we had admired earlier.

When we at first refused to accept, she told us that we could not buy such a carving in the local stores and that because she personally knew an old man in the north of Sweden who made them, she could easily obtain more for herself. The kindness and generosity shown here was replicated on many other occasions throughout my stay.

It was a pleasant experience to observe the warm and spontaneous greeting that we received from all. The children on the street would wave and smile as they said "hei" (hello) to my mother and me. Speaking of children, I spent an entire day with the teachers and children of a day-care centre in Orbyhus—another small community not too far from Tierp. The children were simply fascinated with me. (I don't believe they had had much, if any, contact with a black person before.)

One three-year-old girl kept asking me to repeat Swedish words after her. Finally, when she became convinced that I really did not know Swedish, she said to me (in Swedish, of course), "If you can't speak Swedish, then surely you must speak Finnish." In her small world, people either spoke Swedish or Finnish.

Another nine-year-old boy asked me through an interpreter if I had known Louis Armstrong, who his mother had told him was a great man. He kept talking to me in Swedish for a long time until another girl about his age said to him, "Can't you get it in your head that she speaks *Engleska*, not *Svenska?*" He conceded by telling me to come back and visit them the following year, as by then he would have started to learn English in school.

It was a real joy interacting with these children. In the afternoon, I went along with them for a picnic by a lake. The weather was simply perfect, and although the temperature was only sixty degrees Fahrenheit, with the low humidity, it felt warm and comfortable and more like eighty-degree weather.

One of my more challenging experiences was trying to operate a washing machine, which was located in the basement of the Villa and available for our use. The problem stemmed from the fact that this machine was not like any that I had ever used before, and to make matters worse, all the instructions were in Swedish. Needless to say, I was not able to make head or tail of it and eventually had to appeal to Helvi, the nurse coordinator of the program, for help in operating it.

Because the weekends were free from assignments at the hospital, my mother and I used this opportunity to visit other parts of Sweden and also to take a trip to Finland. For the trip to Finland, we travelled by boat overnight and landed at a town called Turku in Finnish and Abo in Swedish. This is the third largest city in Finland, and it had an interesting history in that it once belonged to Sweden. As a result, the streets still had their Swedish names, as well as their Finnish counterparts. The famous composer Sibelius was born in this city. We went on a city tour in which the tour guide spoke several languages, such as Finnish, Swedish, Russian, German, and lastly, English. Often, by the time she got to English, we would have passed the place being described. Somehow we managed to get by with the brochures. Another place that we visited was a town called Ostersund—a tourist resort in the north of Sweden. This was the kind of place the Swedes would go for a holiday. It was recommended to me by one of the teachers at the day-care centre I mentioned earlier.

We (my mother and I) left Tierp around ten o'clock in the morning and did not arrive in Ostersund until near midnight that day. Although I was a bit anxious, there was no need to be afraid finding my way around. We simply got off the train and, using our map, walked to the Hotel Algen not far from the train station.

The following day, after our arrival in Ostersund, a most unusual incident took place. My mother and I were visiting a nineteenth-century recreated Swedish village and had just bought a special kind of bread used by the Swedish villagers when they left home to work in the mountains for several days at a time. We were getting ready to make ourselves comfortable and eat this bread when we were approached by two women. They offered us some butter, which they said should be used to complement the taste of the bread. In talking to them, we discovered that they were mother and daughter. The daughter, who was probable in her midforties, had been born in the United States but had returned with her Swedish parents to Sweden at the beginning of the depression in the 1930s. The mother was in her eighties and spoke perfect English. They offered to take us in their car to a nearby island, Froson, where we were able to get a magnificent view of the countryside from a lookout point.

It is my wish and dream that one day in the not-too-distant future, I will again have the opportunity to visit Sweden, a country of which I have pleasant memories.

My Visit to West Africa

~~~~~~

(August 1993)

T
here was an air of excitement and anticipation among the passengers when Air Afrique flight No. 94 departed from J F Kennedy Airport bound for Dakar, Senegal, the first stop on the African continent. For many of these passengers, including my sister Brenda and me, it was an emotional trip to the land of our cultural heritage and ancestors who were brought to the Americas and the Caribbean in the chains of slavery.

Usually, passengers applaud when the plane makes a successful landing at the end of its destination. However, this was the first time that the reverse took place and the applause occurred as the plane lifted off the ground at Kennedy Airport. We were on our way to the motherland.

The trip was sponsored by a Panamanian Alumni Association with more than a third of the fifteen members consisting of Jamaican professionals living in the New York area. It was a two-week trip with plans to visit three West African countries:

Ghana, Cote d'Ivoire (the Ivory Coast), and Senegal. Each country was unique and different.

Ghana, however, was very special to me and the other Jamaicans because we were told that many Africans sent to Jamaica originated from a village named Kromantin. Furthermore, I was informed by the tour guide that based on my physical features and stature, I belong to the Ashanti tribe. Indeed I saw many people in Ghana who looked like some of my relatives and fellow Jamaicans.

The Ashantis are ambitious, hard-working, and gregarious people with a firm belief in equality between both sexes. As a matter of fact, no history of Ghana can be written without including the Ashantis. Their culture is influenced by a number of myths and legends, which still exist today. The king of the Ashantis is King Prempeh II, who reigns from the symbolical Golden Stool, which is believed to hold the spirits of all Ashantis. During the period when the slave trade existed in Ghana, the ruling king of the Ashantis was King Prempeh I. Suddenly, as we were given this information, I remembered as a child in Jamaica that persons who were proud and arrogant were referred to as being *prepeh*. I am convinced that there must be some connection to that King Prempeh.

Women play a very important role among the Ashantis, and no matter how inferior an Ashanti woman may appear to an outside observer, she is the final decisive factor in all the activities of the men and is the judge of what is good or bad for the whole community. Ashantis recognize the wisdom of women; the queen mother (the sister of the king) is responsible for the females of the group, and the king for the men.

The high point of the trip to Ghana was the visit to Cape Coast. There, we saw the huge castles that the European slave masters built with the help of Africans. Four hundred years after the slave trade ended, the dungeons still emanate the stench of death and suffering. The captured Africans were kept segregated, the women in the female dungeons and the men in the male dungeons. It was quite an emotional experience for us as we gathered in a circle inside the darkened female dungeon and witnessed an old woman from the village pouring the traditional libation while she informed the spirits of the ancestors that we had come back home.

We then watched a re-enactment of the capture of Africans bound in chains and herded together for waiting ships, their destination unknown. The door that they passed through from the dungeons to the boats waiting to transport them to the ships was called the door of no return. Even though we knew as we watched that it was a re-enactment and not the real thing, emotions ran high, and there were many tears shed by all. The feeling of intense sadness and grief are indescribable. There was a deep sorrow felt for the pain and suffering experienced by our ancestors. Families were separated forever by the cruelty of man's inhumanity to man. Truly this was a holocaust that did not end at the gas chambers such as Auschwitz and other concentration camps; it was a suffering that never ended and still exists today.

Much of the landscape of Ghana reminded me of Jamaica's countryside with the thatched roof huts in the villages. The sight of people sweeping the yards with brooms made of brambles tied together and the warmth and friendliness of the people made me feel very much at home. The presence of higglers in the marketplace and everyone being busy selling something is startlingly reminiscent of Jamaica's ICI (Informal Commercial Importers).

This trip to West Africa has awakened the need for me to know more about the peoples of that vast continent. The visit to the cultural museum in Accra has instilled in me great pride and empowerment. So much of what we believe to be European has, in actuality, evolved from Africa.

THE AFRICAN PRESENCE IN EUROPE

T his trip was an unusual trip and was rather unique. It involved visiting museums, monuments and Black Madonnas. For ten days in October 2013, my sister Brenda from Canada and I went to Europe, along with a group of fifty people. The trip was entitled the African Heritage Tour in Europe. It was sponsored by Dr. Runoko Rashidi, an African American historian whose passion is researching and educating others about the history of black people throughout the world. I have had the opportunity of traveling with him before to Jordan, Morocco, Peru, and Turkey. The trip to Europe involved visiting London (England), Amsterdam (Holland), Brussels (Belgium), and Luxembourg and Paris (France).

Sheila in Paris

The group consisted of mostly retired black female educational administrators and healthcare professionals, as well as young attorneys, an engineer, nurses, and teachers. They came from all over the United States: California; Florida; New Jersey; New York; Ohio; Pennsylvania; Washington, DC; and even Bermuda. Although hectic, the trip was educational and inspirational. It started out in London, where we visited the renowned British Museum, seeing firsthand the works of art stolen from Egypt and Nigeria by colonial rulers.

There was also a walking tour where we saw many of the institutions, such as the banking and insurance businesses, that were developed and formed on the labor of slavery in the Caribbean. We learnt that black history is celebrated in England during the month of October unlike the United States, which celebrates it in February. The walking tour was led by a second-generation Barbadian who informed us of the history of racism in Britain and the efforts taken to resist it. It was evident that Jamaicans have played an important role in preserving their heritage and have made significant contributions to Britain in the area of the healthcare profession and the transportation system.

The next city that we visited was Amsterdam, Holland, a short flight from Gatwick Airport in England. Even though I have been to all the cities on this trip, this time they were viewed from a different perspective. Holland, also known as the Netherlands, is below sea level, and there are many canals throughout the city of Amsterdam. Everybody gets around predominantly by bicycle. They have the right of way, so we had to be very careful when crossing the streets. There are bicycles everywhere that can be rented, very much similar to what Mayor Bloomberg has instituted in New York City. A ride along the canals by boat enabled us to see the houses built from the wealth obtained from the slave trade in the Dutch West Indies. The tour was led by two women who were doing graduate studies involving generations of the Caribbean immigrant population from Surinam and Curacao.

After leaving Amsterdam by coach, we visited a town called Breda in the south of the Netherlands near the border with Belgium. There, we were welcomed by three black women—two of them originally from Surinam and Curacao and the third from the Cameroon in Africa. We heard from them about the struggles they endure as minority women in the Netherlands and their efforts to overcome the prejudices.

Model of a slave ship in Amsterdam

Man carving in the Museum in Brussels

Street scene in Amsterdam

The woman from the Cameroon is an editor who has created a magazine similar to *Ebony* in the United States. This media is used to feature articles that describe the beauty and strength of black women. All three women shared their life stories and entertained us with poetry and music and also provided us with a delicious meal. The encounter with them was heart-warming and brought tears to the eyes of many. We heard of the efforts to discontinue the racist Christmastime tradition of *Zwarte Piet* (Black Pete), which was introduced in a storybook written in 1845 and has since then been celebrated throughout Holland. This practice welcomes the arrival of *Sinterklaas* (Dutch word for *Santa Claus*) on a flying white horse; he is surrounded by his black helper of African origin. Each year on December 5, the morning before the feast of Saint Nicholas, children all over the country wake up excited for gifts and candy while thousands of adults go to their mirrors to apply brown paint and red lips. In their Zwarte Piet costumes, they fill central Amsterdam and small village streets, ushering the arrival of Sinterklaas, much like a Macy's Day parade in the United States.

Cameroon Woman in Breda

In Brussels, we were given a tour of the city where the headquarters for UNESCO and the European Union was established in 1996 and where the office also works in cooperation with other UN bodies present in Brussels, the World Customs Organization, and NATO. A visit to the African Museum involved a very informative lecture given by a cultural anthropologist. She spoke about the reign of terror in the Belgian Congo and how King Leopold of Belgium used the museum to celebrate the Belgian achievement against the African savages. The museum not only displays the stormy pages of history but also provides vast information of the natural history of the Congo. This information has inspired me to learn more about the Congo, which is one of the richest countries in the area of mineral resources yet among the poorest in material wealth in the world.

African Museum in Brussels. Belgium

In Luxembourg, we saw one of the many Black Madonnas in Europe at Saint John's Church. Dr. Rashidi explained that iconic vestiges of the early African imprint on emerging Christianity are shown most strikingly in the hundreds of figurines of the Black Madonna and Child throughout Europe. There can be no doubt that the Black Madonna and Child were derived from the Egyptian gods of Isis and Horus. Even today, the shrines of the Black Madonna are among the holiest and most deeply revered shrines in Europe. They are thought to be miracle workers, and their miracle-working powers are derived from their blackness.

The remaining days of the trip concluded with a train ride from Brussels to Paris, where we went on a city tour, including the Eiffel Tower, the Notre Dame Cathedral, the Arc de Triumph, and of course, a tour of the Louvre Museum. This was my second time to the Louvre, which is a vast museum and would require several visits to make even a dent in seeing everything. I must mention that the weather during this trip was surprisingly warm for this time of year, and only the day after returning to the United States, we learned that there was a hurricane and terrible winds in Europe. We were truly blessed and highly favored.

Black Madonna inside the church in Paris, France

Sheila in Breda, Netherlands

Sheila on vacation in Brussels

VISIT TO VIETNAM AND CAMBODIA

(October 2012)

During the last few weeks in March 2014, all eyes were glued to the television, watching the search and report about the missing Malaysian flight 370. I couldn't help but think about my trip to the neighboring countries of Vietnam and Cambodia in October 2012. My heart goes out to the families of the missing 239 people on board believed to be lost in the Indian Ocean. People ask me if I plan to travel again. My response is yes. The reason for that is my faith in Jesus Christ, who is my protector and shield. If I should die in a plane crash, I know that I would be absent from the body but present with the Lord.

Just a few weeks before my trip to Vietnam and Cambodia was planned, Hurricane Sandy hit us in Canarsie, Brooklyn, New York, on October 29, 2012. Despite the chaos and disruption it caused, I decided that I would still go ahead with my planned vacation and left for Vietnam on November 18. Because my sister Brenda, who was accompanying me on the trip, was leaving from Canada and I from New York, we agreed to meet each other in Hanoi, North Vietnam. She would fly from Toronto to Hong Kong then on to Hanoi. I would fly from New York to Seoul, Korea, then on to Hanoi.

It was a long flight involving a total of fourteen hours, including the stopover in Seoul. On the flight, I sat next to a couple from Queens returning to Cambodia after several years since escaping the terrors of the Pol Pot regime. They were planning to visit relatives they had not seen in many years and would later be joined there by an adult son who was returning for the first time since leaving Cambodia as a child. We went our separate ways after Seoul. I continued to Hanoi, and they continued to Phnom Penh, the capital of Cambodia. When I told them that I planned to visit Cambodia, they said maybe they would see me there. To my surprise, I saw them not in Cambodia but in Vietnam, at the same restaurant where my travel group was having lunch. We hugged each other like long-lost friends. I took a picture of them and promised to contact them when I returned to New York.

By the time I arrived in Hanoi, it was late at night. I was the only person of color on the flight, and as I came through customs and approached the exit, I saw a tour guide holding a sign that indicated she was my travel agent representative. As I walked towards the exit from the building, I was surprised when a group of local people standing there shouted out to me words of welcome to Vietnam. Maybe they thought I was a celebrity like Oprah Winfrey.

The traffic in Hanoi was unbelievably hazardous, with literally hundreds of cars and scooters everywhere. Crossing the street was quite a challenge, yet despite this, there was little evidence of accidents. People seem to know how to cross without getting hit. The drivers seem to move about without displaying annoyance or anger at pedestrians. An interesting observation is the wearing of facial masks by the drivers. We were told that many cover their face to prevent getting sunburnt because white skin is preferred.

Most of our outings around the city and countryside were in comfortable minibuses on land and in boats on the river. One of the highlights of the tour was a visit to Ha Long Bay, one of Southeast Asia's premier tourist destinations. It involved spending a day and overnight trip on a traditional wooden junk boat where we had a seafood lunch and dinner and a pleasant night in a charming cabin. We cruised quietly through the spectacular limestone formations of Ha Long Bay. Upon returning to Hanoi that evening, we enjoyed a night out and watched the Water Puppets Show, which displayed a unique Vietnamese traditional art form.

The shopping in Vietnam is fabulous for those who enjoy shopping and bargains. At one of the cities, silk suits, dresses, and coats can be purchased and custom-made to order. Shoes and boots can also be custom-made for individuals.

One day, we stopped at a huge store where victims of the horrible Agent Orange used in the Vietnam War are trained to make and sell items of clothing, jewelry, food stuff, local paintings, and arts and crafts galore. The evidence of the war is seen by the presence of disabled older men in wheelchairs, sitting on the sidewalks. The visit to the American War Museum in Saigon, now known as Ho Chi Minh City, was very sad; it depicted the cruelty and horrors of the Vietnam War.

Photo of Sheila in Hanoi, Vietnam

There were pictures displaying the method of torture used against the local people in the countryside. There were messages from various countries worldwide condemning the war. The actual weapons of destruction, such as the planes and bombs, were on display in the yard outside the building.

A visit to the famous Cu Chi tunnels, located northwest of Ho Chi Minh City, was an unusual experience. These tunnels were used as the base from which the Vietnamese mounted their operations of the Tet Offensive in 1968. They consist of more than two hundred kilometres of underground tunnels connecting to underground hideouts, shelters, and entrances to other tunnels. The tunnels are just enough for a person to crawl along, and remember, the Vietnamese were much smaller than the Americans.

They literally played tricks on the minds of the Americans as they would disappear into the ground where tunnels were covered and hidden by tree branches and shrubbery. They would leave footprints that they arranged in such a manner that would really be opposite to the direction the person was moving. They would cook meals early in the mornings when there was the presence of fog so that the smoke would not be detected. In the tunnels were medical clinics and elaborate structures so that people could live underground for long periods. Some of the tunnels extended underground even all the way to the North of Vietnam.

Altogether, my tour group consisted of six people (two Canadian couples, my sister Brenda, and me). We spent eleven days in Vietnam and five in Cambodia, visiting five different cities, staying in comfortable four- and five-star hotels. There were two domestic flights in Vietnam and an international flight to Cambodia because it is a different country. The tour guides on the trip were pleasant, very knowledgeable, and English-speaking. The cities are modern and European in style, as well as influenced by Indian, Chinese, and Japanese cultures. The markets are filled with every imaginable product for sale, such as clothing, household appliances, and food supplies. The weather was pleasant, mostly sunny, with an occasional shower of rain. In the city of Tay Ninh, situated at the outskirts of Ho Chi Minh City is the headquarters of the Cao Dai religion founded in 1926.

Upon our arrival around midday, we saw the fantastic midday mass when thousands of followers fill the hall, wearing colored robes—a symbol of the curious combination of Confucianism, Taoism, Christianity, and Buddhism.

Another place of interest was the boat tour downstream on the Mekong Delta. Here, we had the opportunity to discover the local people's life, observing popcorn and pop rice workshop, rice paper mill, coconut candy mill, and fruit gardens. We went by horse-drawn carriages on a village road before having lunch at a local restaurant. The following day, we would depart from Vietnam and continue the second half of the tour in Cambodia. Although I thoroughly enjoyed my visit to this part of the world, for my comfort level on my next trip, I will arrange to travel with the rest of the group from the onset of the tour.

Brenda and Sheila rafting on Halong Bay, Vietnam

Beautiful garden outside the Cao Dai headquarters in Tay Ninh

Brenda in the area of the Cu Chi tunnels in Vietnam

Followers of the Cao Dai religion inside
their head quarters in Tay Ninh

Royal Palace in Phnom Penh, Cambodia

Sheila in Cambodia posing before Angkor Wat Temple

Street scene in Hanoi, Vietnam

Followers of the Cao Dai religion during a Mid-day Mass

Food supplies in market in Saigon, Vietnam

Inside temple in Saigon

Sheila and Brenda on the boat in Halong Bay, Vietnam

Sheila in front of restaurant in Saigon

Sheila waiting outside the resort hotel in Hoi An , Vietnam

Acknowlegements

I would like to acknowledge the encouragement and support that I received from my friends and family in writing this book. It has taken many years to accomplish my goal. Focusing on the manuscript helped me deal with my recent health challenges. Also, Super Storm Sandy of 2012 resulting in the elevation of my house and the stress of relocation for 13 months.

Special thanks to two of my sisters, Dr. Dulce McFarlane, Motivational Speaker, for additional information about our father; Brenda Solomon, English as a Second Language school teacher for editing; and Dawn Alexander, friend and health caregiver, also for editing the manuscript. Thanks to my friend Mary Braham for recommending Xlibris publishers through Vilma Morales Daley, Ed.M., adjunct lecturer City University of New York, poet and author.

It is my hope that this book will be helpful especially
to the younger members of my family in learning and
appreciating the heritage of our family. To my friends from
far and wide, to my church family, health care professionals,
may you enjoy the contents of this manuscript.

Made in the USA
Middletown, DE
05 October 2023